General Directions

FABRIC

These fifty wedding designs can be cross stitched on any evenweave fabric. The term evenweave means the fabric has the same number of threads (or square blocks of threads) per inch, horizontally and vertically, and that number is called its thread count. The stitched size of a design depends on the number of stitches required and the thread count of the fabric. Use the chart below as a guide to determine the stitched height and width of any design on three popular fabric counts.

	Number of Stitches in Design				
Thread Count	**10**	**20**	**30**	**40**	**50**
14 per inch	¾"	1 ⅜"	2 ⅛"	2 ⅞"	3 ⅝"
16 per inch	⅝"	1 ¼"	1 ⅞"	2 ½"	3 ⅛"
18 per inch	½"	1 ⅛"	1 ⅝"	2 ¼"	2 ¾"
	(measurements are given to the nearest 1/8")				

THREADS, NEEDLES, and BEADS

Our cover designs were stitched with Anchor embroidery floss, but we also give the floss numbers for Coats and DMC. Each company has its own color range, so these suggestions are not perfect color matches, but are appropriate substitutions. Generic color names are given for each floss color in a design; for example, if there is only one green it will be so named, but if there are three greens, they will be labelled lt (light), med (medium), and dk (dark).

Cut floss into comfortable working lengths—we suggest about 18". Two strands of floss are usually used to cross stitch on a 14-count background (although one strand can be used for a softened effect). The surface will be adequately covered by the stitches, yet the delicacy of the pattern is retained. For a more solid color effect, use two strands of floss on 16-count Aida (as shown on our cover stitching). One strand of floss is sufficient to cross stitch on 18-count fabric. Size 24 or 26 blunt-pointed tapestry needles are suitable for these fabrics.

Several designs are embellished with seed beads; use a #28 tapestry or a beading needle to attach them. For added sparkle, optional glass charms have been tacked on with floss or thread. To attach a charm that has a center hole, bring threaded needle up through hole, slip on a seed bead, then stitch back down through same hole; the bead will secure the charm in place.

WORKING FROM CHARTED DESIGNS

Each square on a charted design corresponds to a space for a cross stitch on the stitching surface. The symbol in a square specifies the color to be used for that stitch. The stitch width and height are given for each design, and centers are shown by arrows.

If a color name is given without a symbol, the color is used for one of the following decorative stitches. Backstitches and straight stitches are shown by straight lines and French knots by dots.

GETTING STARTED

To begin in an unstitched area, bring threaded needle to front of fabric. Hold an inch of the end against the back, then anchor it with your first few stitches. To end threads and begin new ones next to existing stitches, weave through the backs of several stitches.

THE STITCHES

Note: Unless otherwise noted in the color key, use two strands of floss for all cross stitches, French knots, and beads, and one strand for backstitches and straight stitches.

Cross Stitch

The cross stitch is formed in two motions. Follow the numbering in **Fig 1** and bring needle up at 1, down at 2, up at 3, down at 4, to complete the stitch. Work horizontal rows of stitches, **Fig 2**, wherever possible. Bring thread up at 1, work half of each stitch across the row, then complete the stitches on your return.

Fig 1 **Fig 2**

Backstitch

Backstitches are worked after cross stitches have been completed. They may slope in any direction and are occasionally worked over more than one square of fabric. **Fig 3** shows the progression of several stitches; bring thread up at odd numbers and down at even numbers.

Sometimes you have to choose where to end one backstitch color and begin the next color. As a rule of thumb, choose the object that should appear closest to you. Backstitch around that shape with the appropriate color, then backstitch the areas behind it with adjacent color(s).

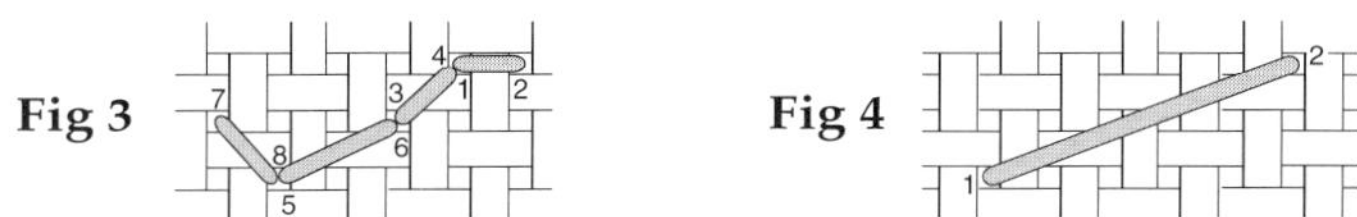

Fig 3 **Fig 4**

Straight Stitch

A straight stitch, **Fig 4**, is made like a long backstitch. Come up at one end of the stitch and down at the other. The length and direction of these stitches will vary—follow the chart for exact placement.

French Knot

Bring thread up where indicated on chart, **Fig 5**. Wrap floss once around needle and reinsert needle close to, but at least one fabric thread away from, where floss emerged. Hold wrapping thread tightly and pull needle and floss through fabric, releasing floss just as knot is formed. For a larger knot, use more strands of floss, but wrap only once.

Fig 5 **Fig 6** **Fig 7**

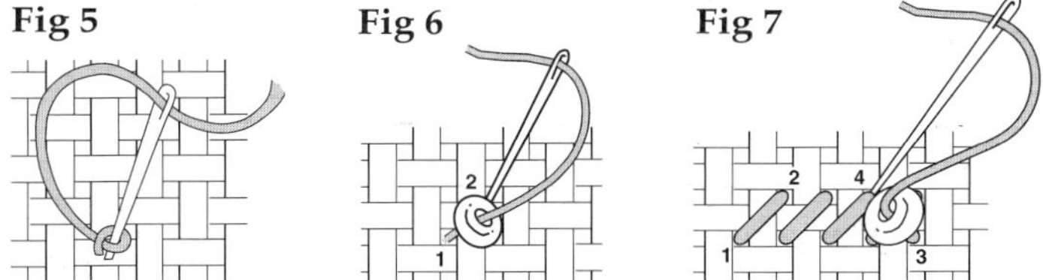

Bead Attachment

We used two methods to attach seed beads: half cross stitches and full cross stitches. For the first, bring floss up at lower left corner of stitch at 1, slip bead on needle, and stitch down at 2, at upper right corner of stitch, **Fig 6**.

For the full cross stitch method, **Fig 7**, work the first half of the row (1-2) from left to right as usual. On the return, pick up each bead as needed, slip it on needle, and stitch down to secure (3-4).

FINISHING

Dampen stitching, or wash with gentle soap in cool water and rinse well. Roll in a towel and squeeze out excess moisture. Place face down on a dry towel or padded surface and iron carefully. Frame or finish as desired.

1 Design size: 41 wide x 29 high

Stitching note: If desired, attach a charm (Mill Hill 13006) with a crystal seed bead over flower on glove.

			Anchor	Coats	DMC
▫	=	white	2	1001	blanc
⟡	=	pink	74	3003	3354
☆	=	lt yellow	386	2386	3823
+	=	med yellow	301	2293	744
★	=	dk yellow	891	5363	676
		gold	1001	2308	976
#	=	lt green	1043	6015	369
		dk green	243	6239	703
△	=	lt blue	128	7031	800
▲	=	med blue	129	7976	809
		dk blue	131	7022	798
~	=	lt tan	366	3335	951
⊙	=	med tan	368	5345	437

| = Backstitch:
yellow flowers, gloves—*gold*
leaves, stems—*dk green*
blue flowers, garter, shoes—*dk blue*

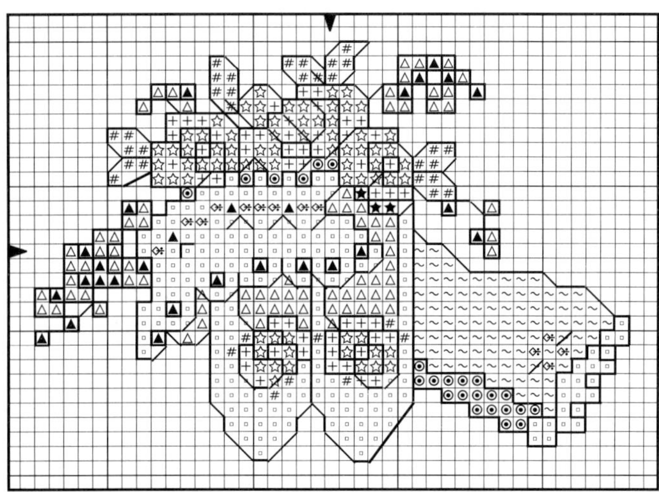

2 Design size: 26 wide x 48 high

			Anchor	Coats	DMC
▫	=	white	2	1001	blanc
○	=	lt pink	36	3125	3326
		dk pink	38	3283	961
~	=	lt peach	6	3006	754
⊙	=	med peach	9	3008	352
◇	=	lt green	1043	6015	369
		dk green	243	6239	703
⟡	=	blue	128	7031	800
♥	=	purple	110	4301	208
		gray	235	8513	414

| = Backstitch:
flowers, heart, scallop trim on cake—*dk pink*
stems, leaves—*dk green*
remaining—*gray*

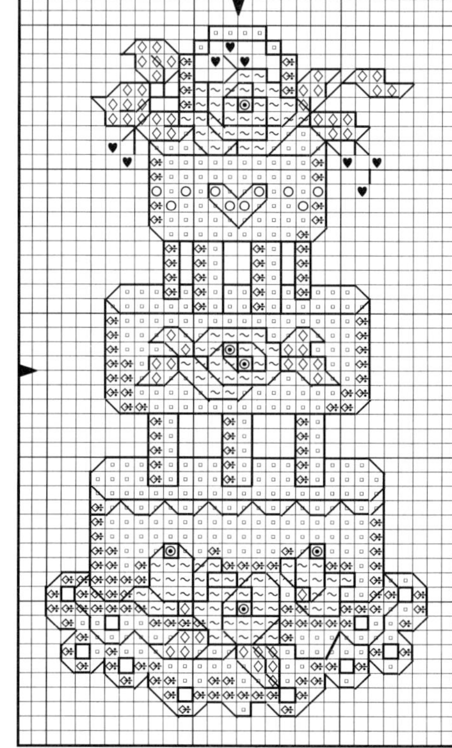

3 Design size: 14 wide (plus names) x 29 high

Stitching note: Use the alphabet on page 17 to work desired names with dk blue. Use gold floss to attach bead with 1/2 cross stitch.

			Anchor	Coats	DMC
▫	=	white	2	1001	blanc
○	=	lt pink	48	3150	3689
⟡	=	med pink	36	3125	3326
		dk pink	39	3154	309
☆	=	yellow	300	2350	745
		gold	365	5365	435
#	=	lt green	240	6016	966
		dk green	243	6239	703
△	=	lt blue	129	7976	809
		dk blue	131	7022	798

Mill Hill Seed Bead

+ = gold 00557

| = Backstitch:
hearts—*dk pink*
stem, bell, string—*gold*
leaves—*dk green*
lettering, blue band on bell—*dk blue*

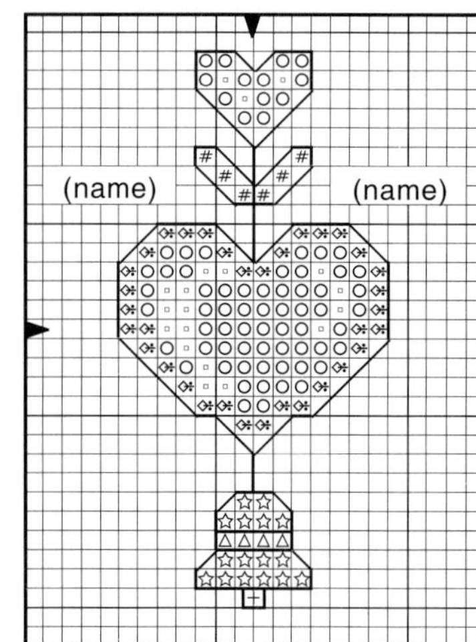

4 Design size: 17 wide x 18 high

			Anchor	Coats	DMC
~	=	lt peach	6	3006	754
⟡	=	med peach	9	3008	352
#	=	green	243	6239	703
–	=	lt purple	103	4303	211
➘	=	med purple	96	4104	3609
		gray	400	8512	317

| = Backstitch: *gray*

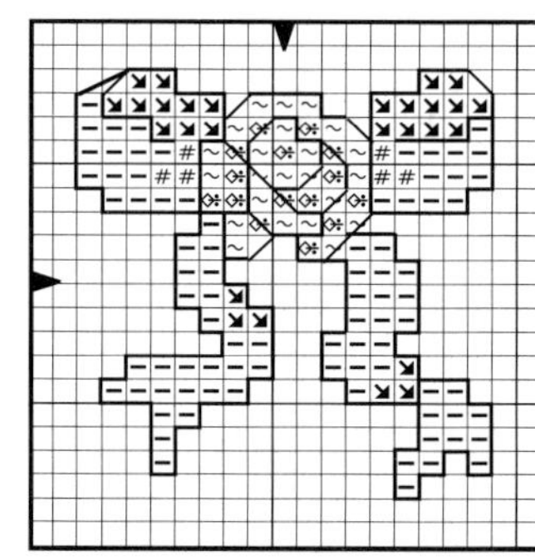

5

Design size: 55 wide x 53 high
Stitching note: Use med green floss to attach beads with cross stitches.

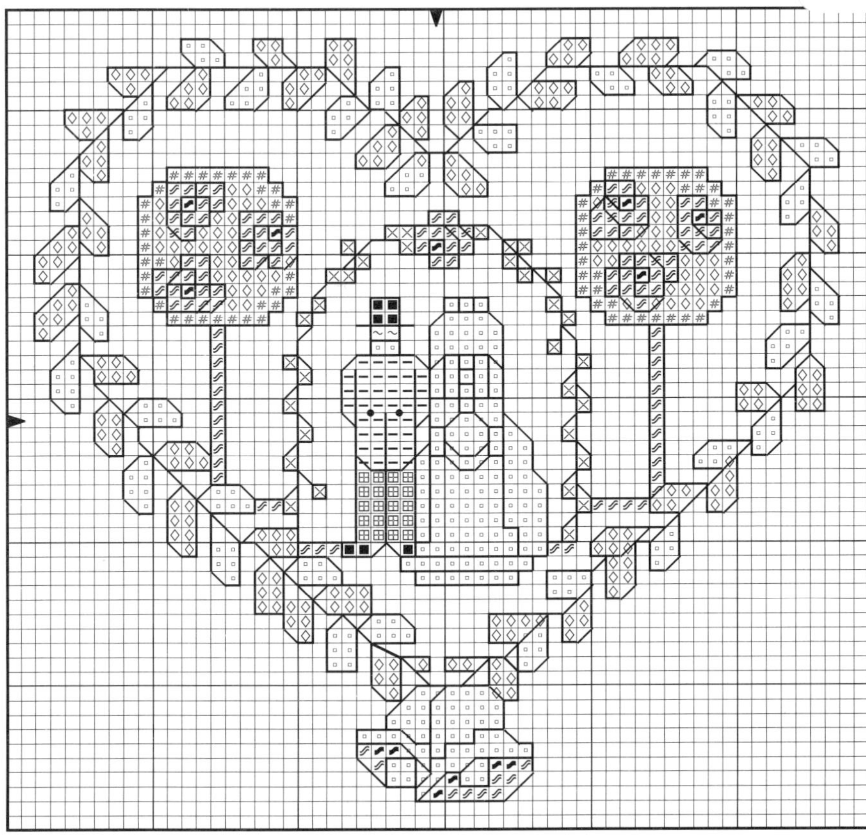

		Anchor	Coats	DMC
▫ =	white	2	1001	blanc
~ =	very lt peach	778	2336	3774
⁄⁄ =	lt peach	6	3006	754
◢ =	med peach	9	3008	352
	dk peach	1024	3071	3328
◇ =	lt green	1043	6015	369
# =	med green	240	6016	966
	dk green	210	6213	562
– =	lt gray	398	8398	415
⊞ =	med gray	235	8513	414
	dk gray	400	8512	317
■ =	very dk gray	236	8514	3799

Mill Hill Seed Beads

× = green 00167

• = French Knots: *dk gray*
| = Backstitch:
flowers, tree trunks—*dk peach*
stems, leaves—*dk green*
bride, groom, bells—*dk gray*

6

Design size: 15 wide x 52 high
Stitching note: Use blue floss to attach beads with cross stitches.

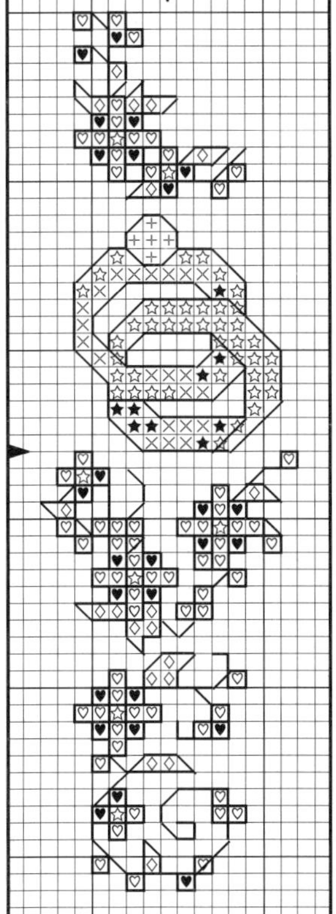

		Anchor	Coats	DMC
☆ =	lt gold	311	2305	3827
× =	med gold	890	2875	729
★ =	dk gold	901	2876	3829
◇ =	lt green	240	6016	966
	dk green	243	6239	703
	blue	128	7031	800
♡ =	lt purple	95	4085	554
♥ =	dk purple	92	4087	553
	gray	235	8513	414

Mill Hill Seed Beads

+ = crystal 02010

| = Backstitch:
rings (except diamond)—*dk gold*
leaves, stems—*dk green*
flowers—*dk purple*
diamond—*gray*

7

Design size: 26 wide x 41 high
Stitching note: If desired, attach a bird charm (Mill Hill 12051) near roof.

		Anchor	Coats	DMC
▫ =	white	2	1001	blanc
× =	fuchsia	85	4085	3609
☆ =	yellow	301	2293	744
	gold	307	5307	783
◇ =	lt green	259	6250	772
# =	med green	261	6266	989
⊕ =	blue	128	7031	800
	gray	400	8512	317

| = Backstitch:
cross—*gold (2 strands)*
remaining outlines—*gray*

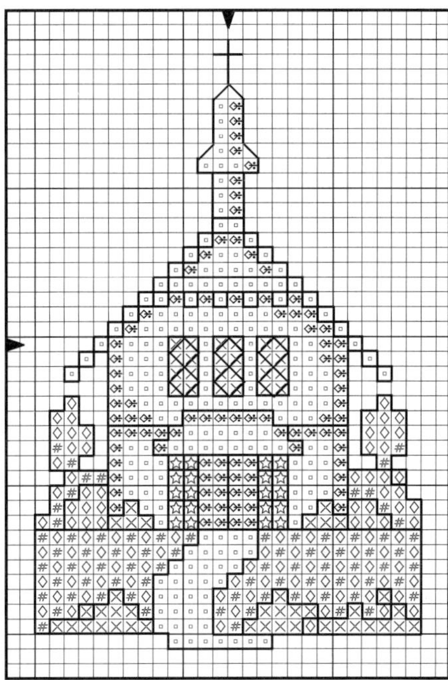

8

Design size: 47 wide x 37 high

Stitching note: If desired, attach a heart charm (Mill Hill 12076) over blue heart between doves.

		Anchor	Coats	DMC
▫ =	white	2	1001	blanc
☆ =	yellow	300	2350	745
# =	lt green	214	6016	368
	dk green	217	6211	561
^ =	lt blue	1031	7031	3753
	dk blue	1034	7051	931
♡ =	lt purple	95	4085	554
♥ =	dk purple	98	4097	553
	brown	370	5356	434

| = Backstitch:
stems—*dk green*
birds, hearts—*dk blue*
lettering—*dk purple*
flowers—*brown*

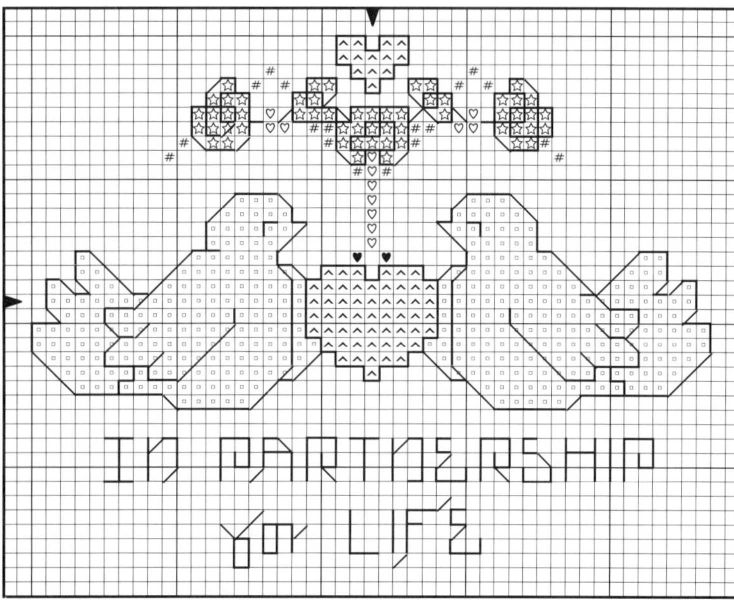

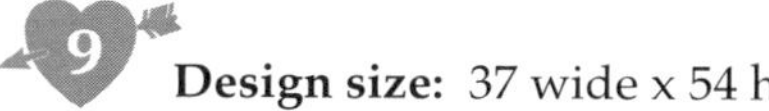

9

Design size: 37 wide x 54 high

		Anchor	Coats	DMC
▫ =	white	2	1001	blanc
− =	lt pink	48	3150	3689
⊹ =	med pink	36	3125	3326
⁄ =	lt peach	778	2336	3774
◢ =	med peach	868	3868	353
☆ =	yellow	301	2293	744
★ =	gold	890	2875	729
◇ =	green	240	6016	966
+ =	lt blue	128	7031	800
↘ =	med blue	129	7976	809
	brown	370	5356	434
	gray	235	8513	414

| = Backstitch:
face (except eye), arms, hair, yellow flowers—*brown*
eye—*gray (2 strands)*
remaining outlines—*gray*

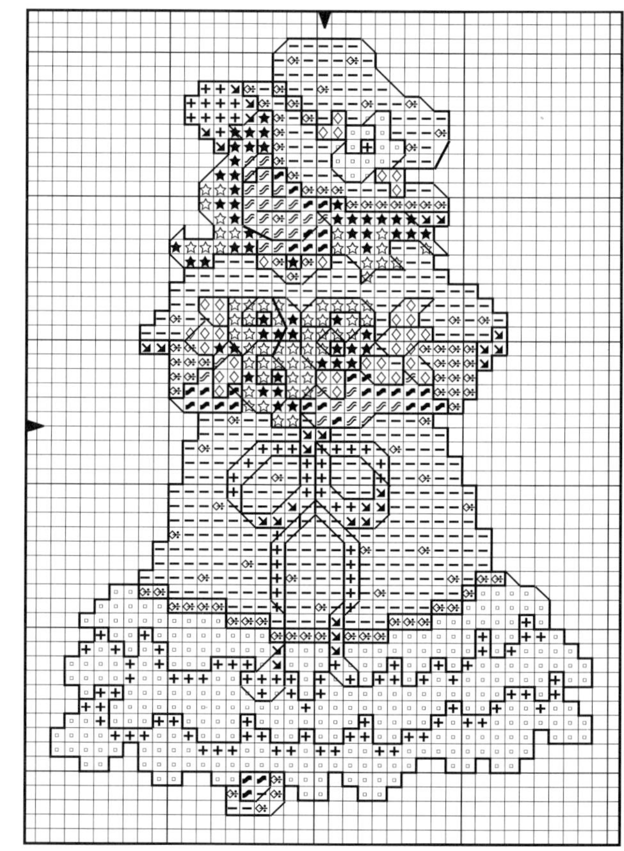

10

Design size: 17 wide x 29 high

		Anchor	Coats	DMC
☆ =	lt yellow	300	2350	745
+ =	med yellow	311	2305	3827
★ =	dk yellow	890	2875	729
↘ =	brown	370	5356	434

| = Backstitch:
chain—*dk yellow*
key, lock—*brown*

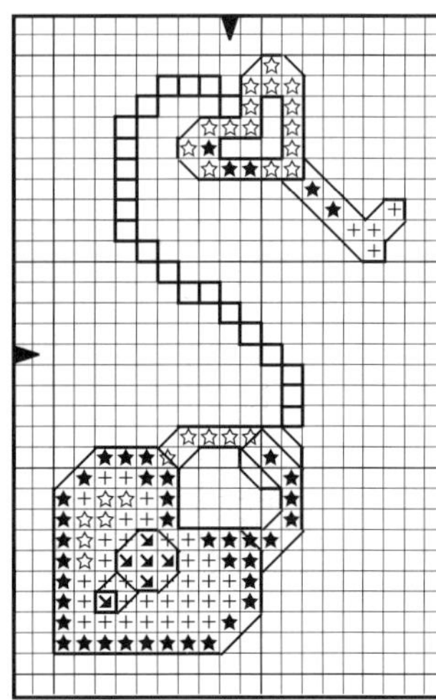

11

Design size: 30 wide x 24 high

		Anchor	Coats	DMC
▫ =	white	2	1001	blanc
○ =	lt pink	48	3150	3689
⊹ =	med pink	36	3125	3326
☆ =	lt gold	311	2305	3827
× =	med gold	890	2875	729
★ =	dk gold	901	2876	3829
	very dk gold	309	5309	781
	green	210	6213	562
△ =	lt blue	128	7031	800
▲ =	med blue	129	7976	809
	dk blue	131	7022	798

| = Backstitch:
rings—*very dk gold*
stems—*green*
flowers, ribbon—*dk blue*

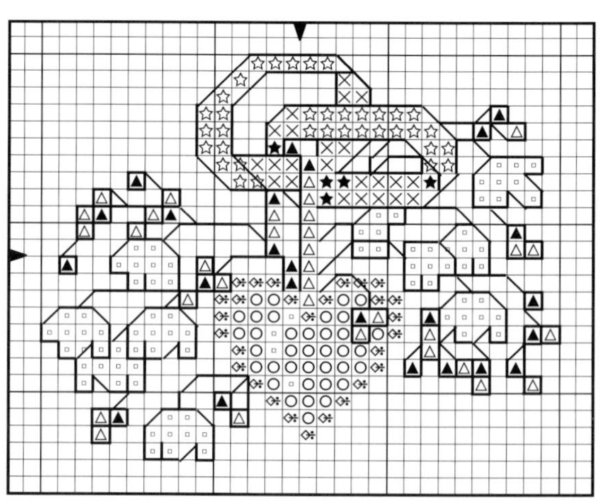

12

Design size: 51 wide x 51 high
Stitching note: Use one strand of white floss to attach beads at intersections on headpiece with 1/2 cross stitches.

Symbol		Color	Anchor	Coats	DMC
▫	=	white	2	1001	blanc
━	=	lt pink	271	3280	819
♡	=	med pink	24	3281	963
♥	=	dk pink	76	3176	961
#	=	green	206	6209	564
=	=	lt blue	128	7031	800
◈	=	med blue	129	7976	809
∮	=	lt tan	366	3335	951
◢	=	med tan	368	5345	437
		med gray	235	8513	414
■	=	dk gray	400	8512	317

Mill Hill Seed Beads

• = white 00479

| = Backstitch:
lettering—*dk pink*
remaining outlines—*med gray*

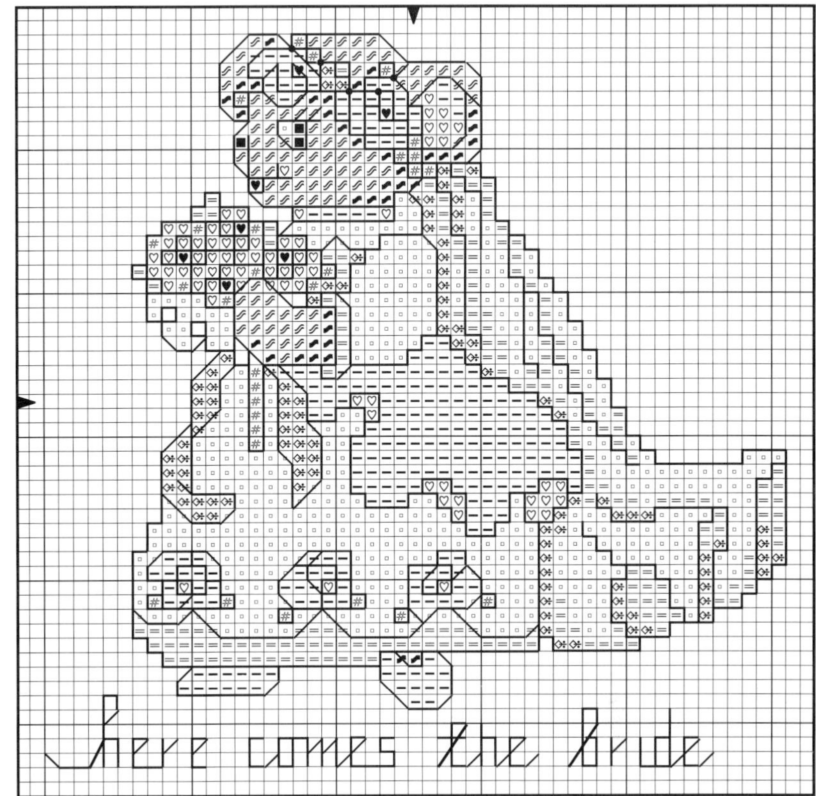

13

Design size: 55 wide x 52 high
Stitching note: Backstitch the square outlines around beads, then use one strand of white floss to attach beads with 1/2 cross stitches.

Symbol		Color	Anchor	Coats	DMC
▫	=	white	2	1001	blanc
○	=	lt pink	48	3150	3689
◈	=	med pink	36	3125	3326
●	=	dk pink	38	3283	961
✱	=	med gold	1002	2306	977
		dk gold	365	5365	435
◇	=	lt green	1043	6015	369
#	=	med green	240	6016	966
◆	=	dk green	242	6225	989
		very dk green	210	6213	562
△	=	lt blue	128	7031	800
⊕	=	med blue	129	7976	809
		dk blue	131	7022	798
~	=	very lt tan	276	5533	739
□	=	lt tan	367	5375	738
✕	=	med tan	368	5345	437
■	=	brown	359	5472	801
		gray	235	8513	414

Mill Hill Seed Beads

+ = white pearl 00479

\ = Straight Stitch: *gray*
| = Backstitch:
pink flowers, hearts—*dk pink*
frame—*dk gold*
leaves, stems—*very dk green*
veil, fringe on dress, pin stripes on groom's vest & button, blue flowers, lettering—*dk blue*
faces—*brown*
remaining dress, bead outlines, shirt, tie, vest, banner—*gray*

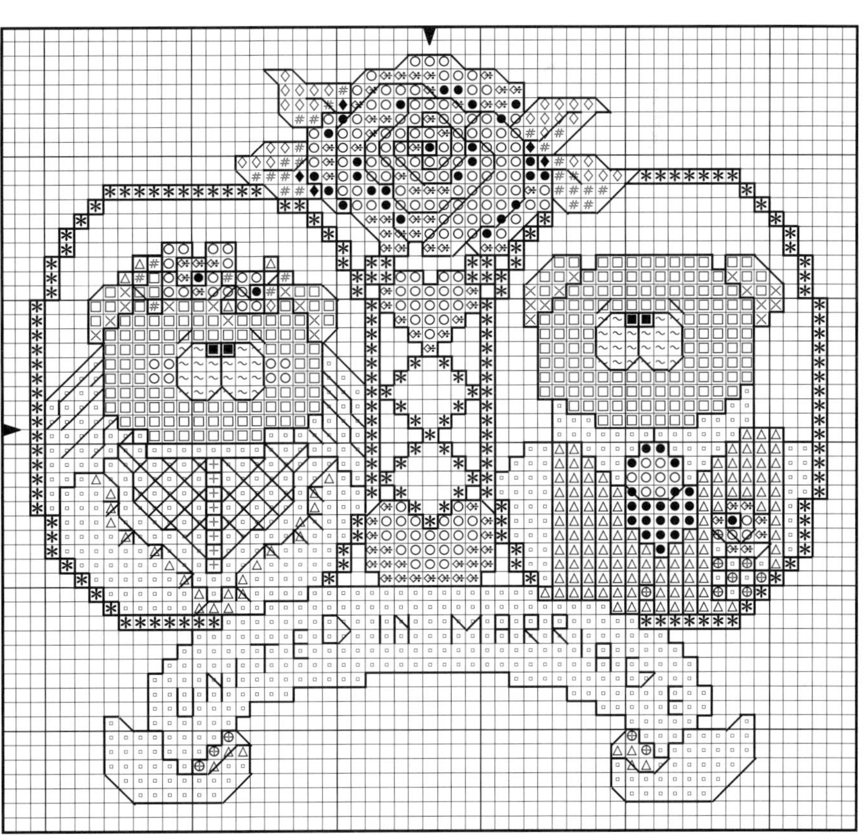

14 Design size: 46 wide x 50 high

		Anchor	Coats	DMC
▫ =	white	2	1001	blanc
☆ =	yellow	300	2350	745
★ =	med gold	1002	2306	977
	dk gold	1049	5349	3826
◇ =	lt green	240	6016	966
◆ =	med green	242	6225	989
◘ =	dk green	227	6227	701
~ =	very lt blue	128	7031	800
○ =	lt blue	129	7976	3325
⊙ =	med blue	130	7021	809
	gray	400	8512	317

| = Backstitch:
inside lily petals, stamen, lettering—*dk gold*
leaves, stems—*dk green*
flower outlines, banner—*gray*

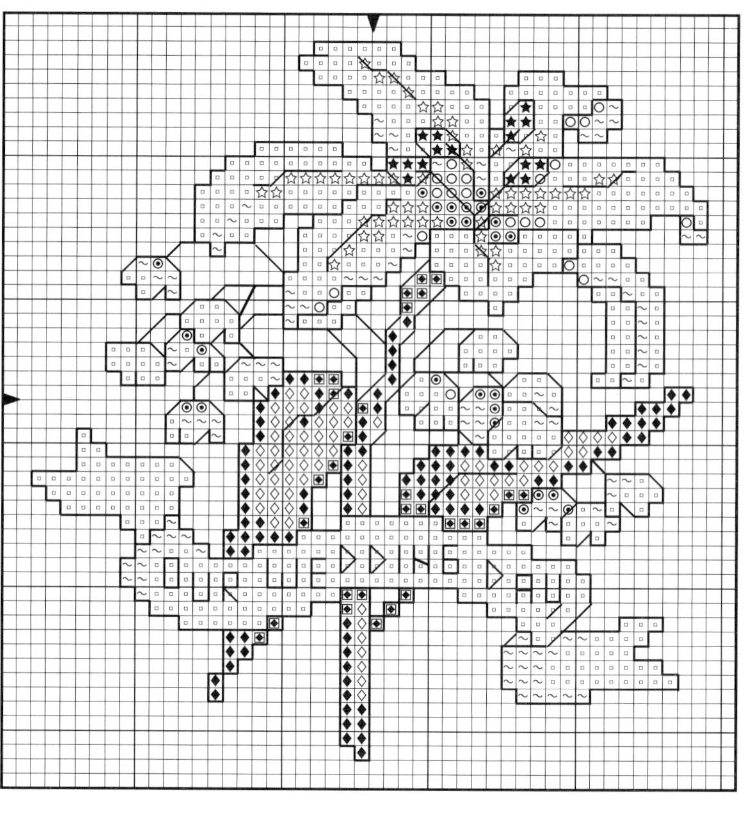

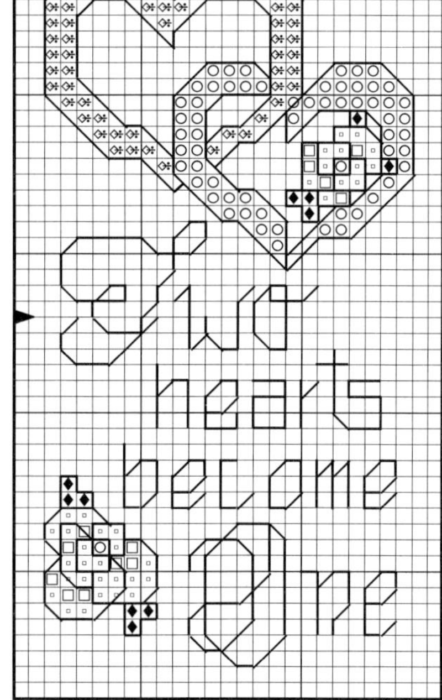

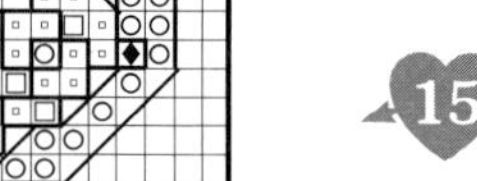

15 Design size: 23 wide x 44 high

		Anchor	Coats	DMC
▫ =	white	2	1001	blanc
○ =	lt pink	1021	3068	761
⊕ =	med pink	895	3241	223
	dk pink	1027	2342	3722
◆ =	med green	214	6016	368
	dk green	216	6876	502
□ =	lt blue	128	7031	800
	dk blue	131	7022	798

| = Backstitch:
hearts, lettering—*dk pink*
leaves—*dk green*
flowers—*dk blue*

16 Design size: 44 wide x 44 high

		Anchor	Coats	DMC
▫ =	white	2	1001	blanc
~ =	lt peach	6	3006	754
⊕ =	med peach	9	3008	352
◢ =	dk peach	11	3111	351
☆ =	lt gold	311	2305	3827
× =	med gold	890	2875	729
★ =	dk gold	901	2876	3829
□ =	lt blue	128	7031	800
∞ =	med blue	130	7021	809
■ =	dk blue	131	7022	798
^ =	lt rust	1047	5347	402
⊙ =	med rust	1048	3336	3776
	gray	400	8512	317

• = French Knots: *gray*
| = Backstitch:
flowers—*dk peach*
bells, ribbon—*gray*

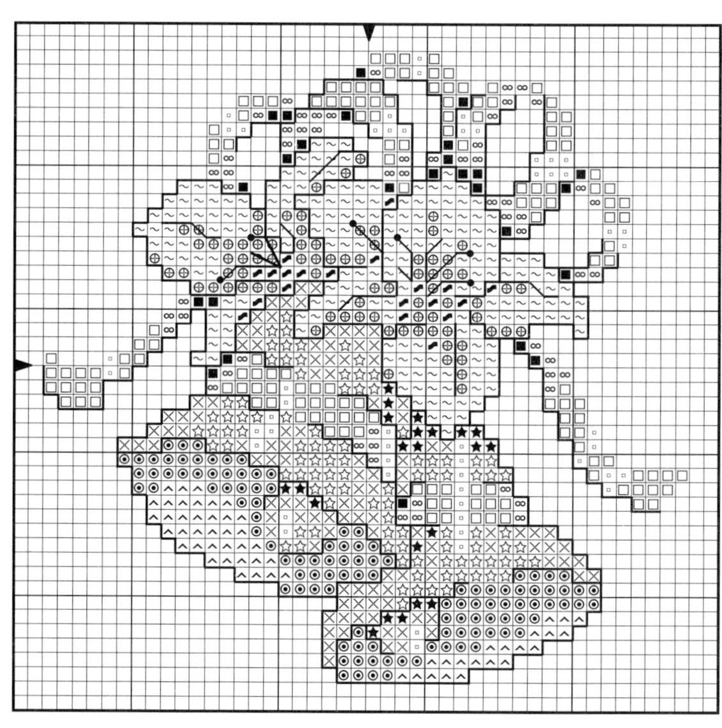

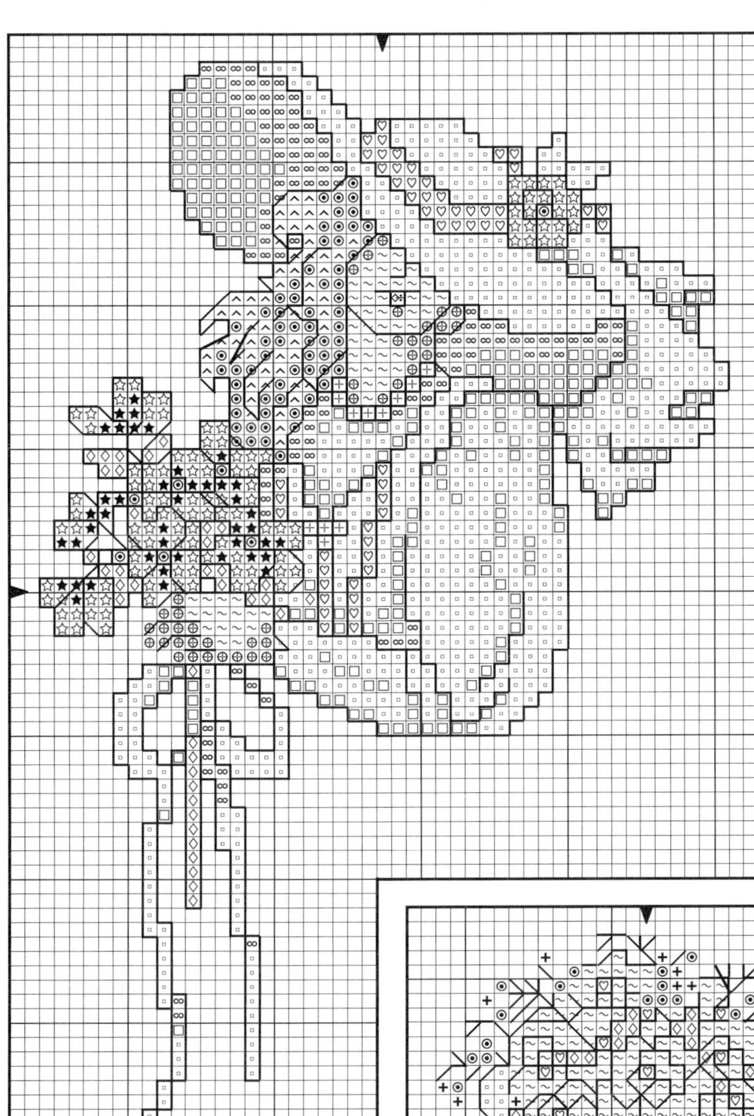

17 **Design size:** 47 wide x 74 high

Stitching note: Backstitch the square outlines around beads, then use white floss to attach beads with 1/2 cross stitches.

			Anchor	Coats	DMC
▫	=	white	2	1001	blanc
◇•	=	pink	38	3283	961
~	=	lt peach	778	2336	3774
⊕	=	med peach	868	3868	353
☆	=	lt yellow	300	2350	745
★	=	med yellow	891	5363	676
◇	=	lt green	240	6016	966
		dk green	258	6258	905
□	=	lt blue	128	7031	800
∞	=	med blue	129	7976	809
♡	=	lt purple	342	4303	211
♥	=	med purple	109	4302	209
^	=	lt rust	1047	5347	402
⊙	=	med rust	1048	3336	3776
		dk rust	351	3340	400
		gray	235	8513	414

Mill Hill Seed Beads

+ = pearl white 00479

| = Backstitch:
leaves, stems—*dk green*
hair, skin, flowers—*dk rust*
hat, veil, bead outlines, dress, ribbon—*gray*

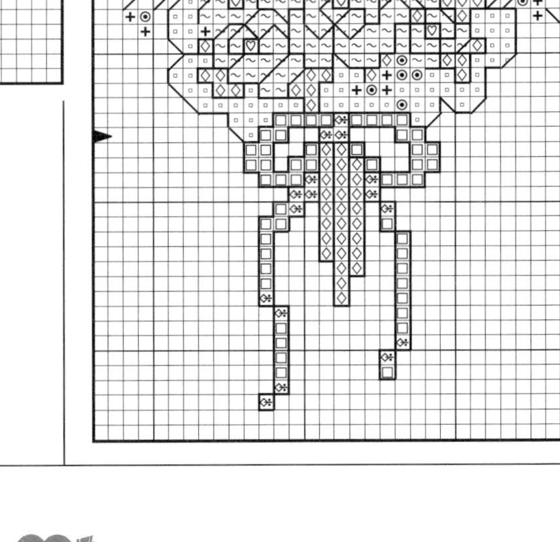

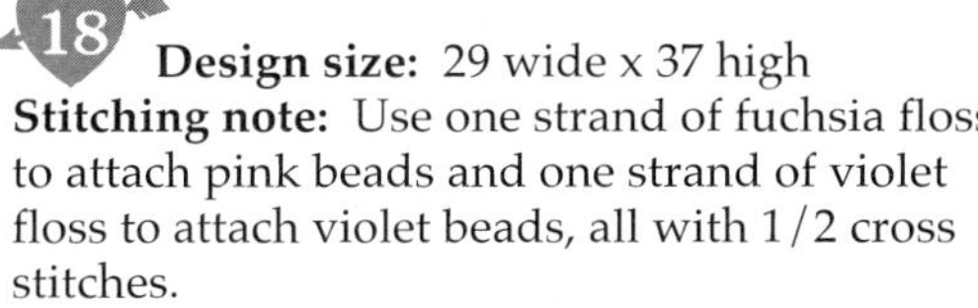

18 **Design size:** 29 wide x 37 high

Stitching note: Use one strand of fuchsia floss to attach pink beads and one strand of violet floss to attach violet beads, all with 1/2 cross stitches.

			Anchor	Coats	DMC
▫	=	white	2	1001	blanc
~	=	lt pink	48	3150	3689
♡	=	med pink	36	3125	3326
		dk pink	38	3283	961
		fuchsia	86	4086	3608
◇	=	lt green	206	6209	564
		dk green	243	6239	703
□	=	lt blue	128	7031	800
◇•	=	med blue	130	7021	809
		violet	109	4302	209
		gray	235	8513	414

Mill Hill Seed Beads

+ = pink 00553

⊙ = violet 02009

| = Backstitch:
flowers—*dk pink*
stems, leaves—*dk green*
doily, ribbon—*gray*

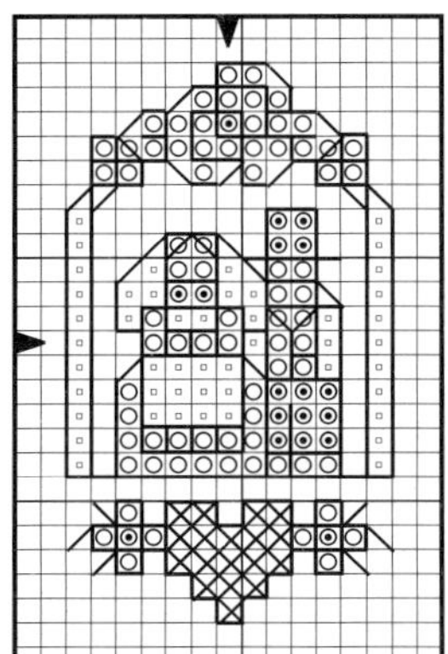

19 **Design size:** 13 wide x 23 high

			Anchor	Coats	DMC
▫	=	white	2	1001	blanc
○	=	lt blue	128	7031	800
⊙	=	med blue	939	7005	794
		dk blue	940	7022	792

| = Backstitch: *dk blue*

20

Design size: 111 wide x 20 high
Stitching note: Use white floss to attach crystal beads and lt blue floss to attach blue beads, all with 1/2 cross stitches.

		Anchor	Coats	DMC
▫ =	white	2	1001	blanc
♡ =	lt fuchsia	95	4085	554
+ =	med fuchsia	96	4104	3609
	dk fuchsia	92	4087	553
~ =	lt gold	311	2305	3827
✱ =	med gold	890	2875	729
	dk gold	1001	2308	976
♦ =	med green	242	6225	989
	dk green	210	6213	562
□ =	lt blue	129	7976	809
	dk blue	131	7022	798

Mill Hill Seed Beads

○ =	crystal	02010
× =	blue	02006

| = Backstitch:
fuchsia ribbon—*dk fuchsia*
ring (except diamonds), gold
leaves, stems—*dk green*
bead outlines, flowers, letterin
diamonds—*dk blue*

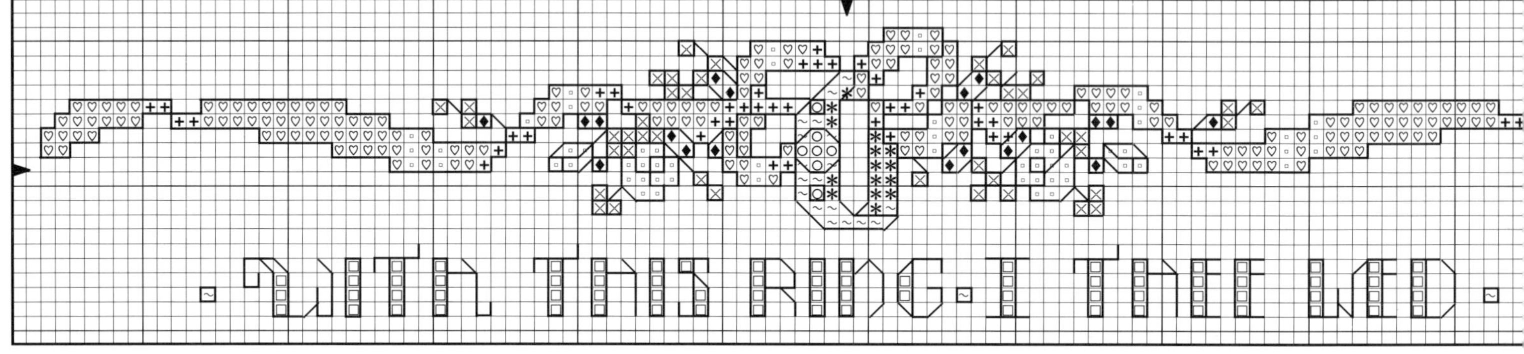

21

Design size: 54 wide x 75 high
Stitching note: Backstitch the square outlines around beads, then use ivory floss to attach beads with cross stitches.

		Anchor	Coats	DMC
▫ =	ivory	275	2275	746
⊛ =	pink	36	3125	3326
− =	very lt peach	880	3335	3774
⫽ =	lt peach	881	2331	945
◤ =	med peach	882	2337	758
^ =	lt yellow	885	2386	739
○ =	med yellow	886	5372	677
◇ =	lt green	261	6266	989
♦ =	med green	243	6239	703
□ =	lt blue	128	7031	800
# =	med blue	129	7976	809
♡ =	med purple	110	4301	208
♥ =	dk purple	112	4300	552
◢ =	tan	368	5345	437
= =	lt rust	1047	5347	402
☆ =	med rust	1048	3336	3776
★ =	dk rust	1049	5349	3826
	gray	400	8512	317
	black	403	8403	310

Mill Hill Seed Beads

+ =	pearl	00479
× =	cream	00123

| = Backstitch:
face (except eye), neck, hands, veil, dress, cream bead outlines—*dk rust*
hair, flowers, pearl bead outlines, ribbon—*gray*
eye—*black (2 strands)*

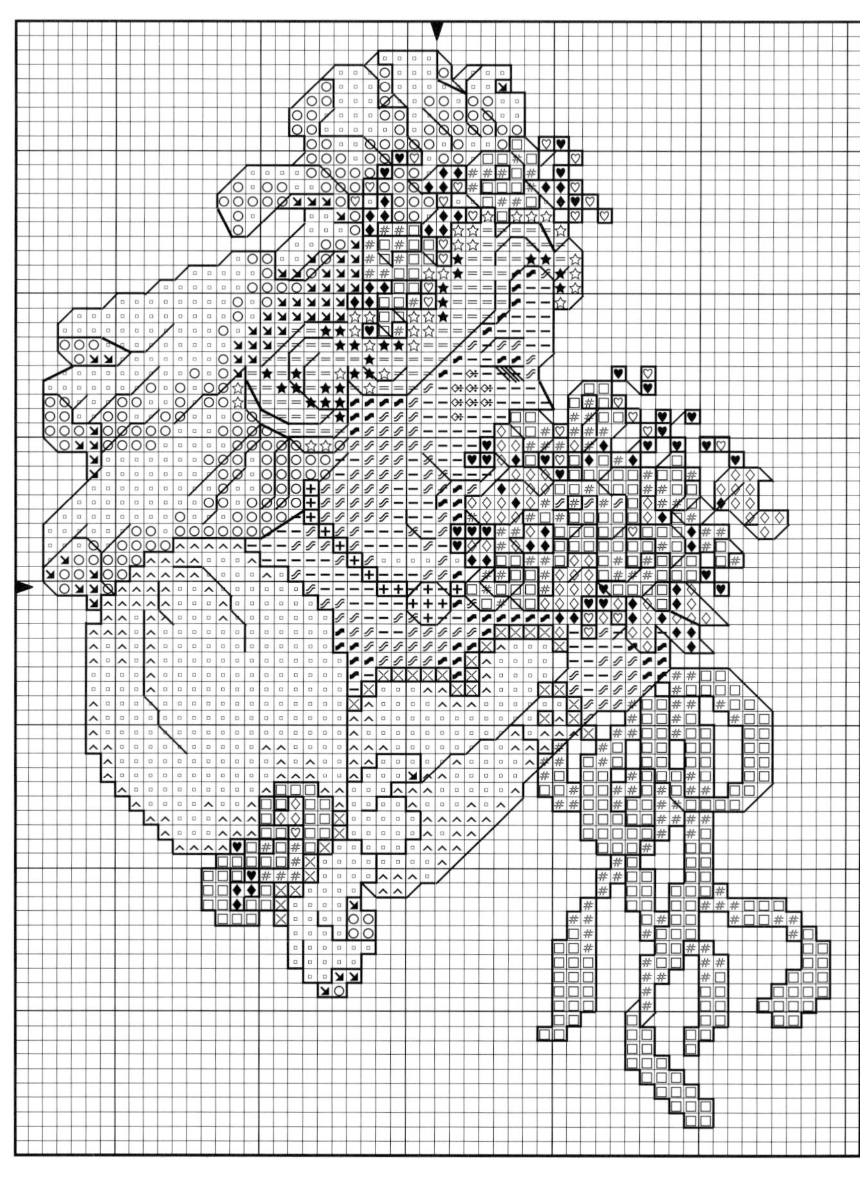

23

D
Stitching
outlines a
floss to at
stitches.

▫ = whi
~ = lt pe
⊙ = mec
☆ = lt ye
★ = mec
△ = lt bl
▲ = mec
dk b
brow

+ = pear

| = Bac
beac
flow

gold

22 **Design size:** 45 wide x 95 high

Stitching note: Backstitch the square outlines around beads, then use white floss to attach beads with 1/2 cross stitches.

			Anchor	Coats	DMC
▫	=	white	2	1001	blanc
▬	=	lt pink	48	3150	3689
♡	=	med pink	36	3125	3326
♥	=	dk pink	38	3283	961
~	=	very lt peach	6	3006	754
⫽	=	lt peach	8	3868	3824
▰	=	med peach	9	3008	352
^	=	very lt yellow	300	2350	745
☆	=	lt yellow	301	2293	744
★	=	med yellow	891	5363	676
		gold	901	2876	3829
◇	=	lt green	1043	6015	369
#	=	med green	240	6016	966
		dk green	210	6213	562
×	=	blue	128	7031	800
=	=	very lt purple	95	4085	554
△	=	lt purple	96	4104	3609
▲	=	med purple	98	4097	553
		gray	235	8513	414

Mill Hill Seed Beads

\+ = mauve 00151

| = Backstitch:
pink & peach tulips, hearts, lettering—*dk pink*
yellow tulips—*gold*
stems—*dk green*
purple tulips, white flowers, bead outlines, banner—*gray*

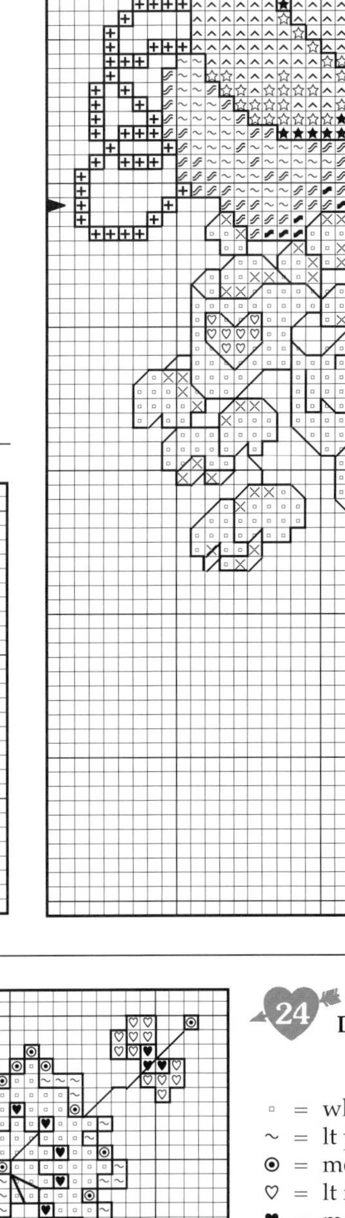

e: 28 wide x 26 high
ackstitch the square
eads, then use white
ds with 1/2 cross

nchor	Coats	DMC
2	1001	blanc
6	3006	754
9	3008	352
300	2350	745
891	5363	676
128	7031	800
130	7021	809
131	7022	798
370	5356	434

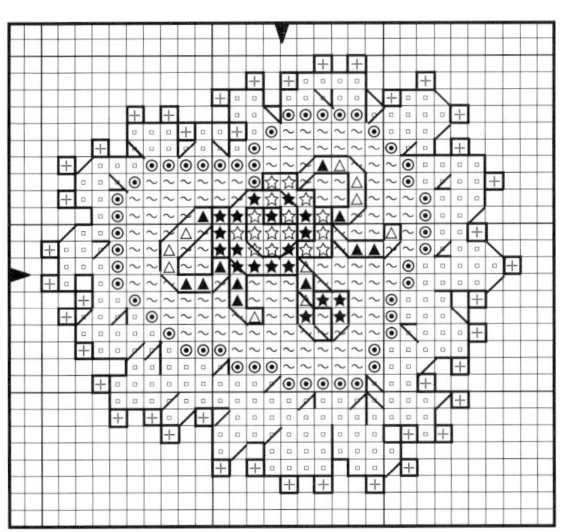

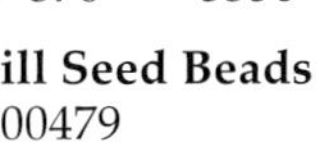

Hill Seed Beads
00479

s, lace, bow—*dk blue*
—*brown*

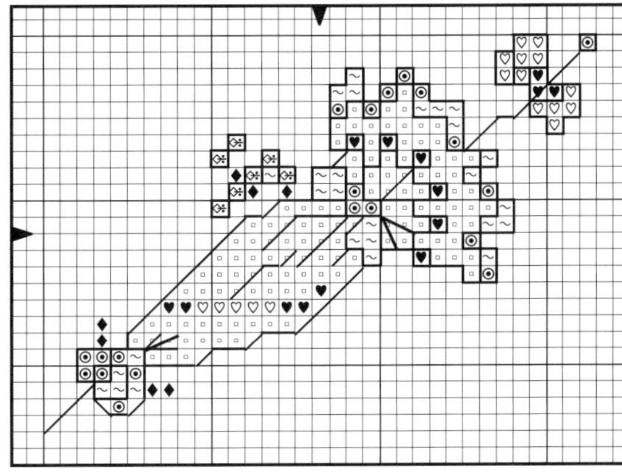

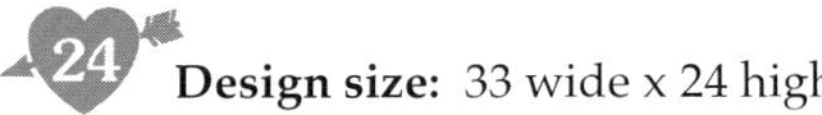

24 **Design size:** 33 wide x 24 high

			Anchor	Coats	DMC
▫	=	white	2	1001	blanc
~	=	lt peach	6	3006	754
⊙	=	med peach	9	3008	352
♡	=	lt fuchsia	96	4104	3609
♥	=	med fuchsia	97	4097	554
♦	=	green	214	6016	368
⟴	=	blue	129	7976	809
		gray	235	8513	414

\ = Straight Stitch (base of ruffle): *gray*

| = Backstitch: *gray*

25

Design size: 43 wide x 34 high
Stitching note: Backstitch the square outlines around beads, then use white floss to attach beads with 1/2 cross stitches.

		Anchor	Coats	DMC
▫ =	white	2	1001	blanc
○ =	lt pink	48	3150	3689
● =	dk pink	38	3283	961
◇ =	lt green	1043	6015	369
	dk green	243	6239	703
△ =	lt turquoise	185	6185	964
▲ =	med turquoise	187	6186	958
~ =	lt blue	128	7031	800
⊙ =	med blue	129	7976	809
	gray	235	8513	414

Mill Hill Seed Beads

+ = pearl 00479

| = Backstitch:
connecting lines on lace, garter stripes—*dk pink*
leaves—*dk green*
bead outlines, remaining garter, rose, ribbon—*gray*

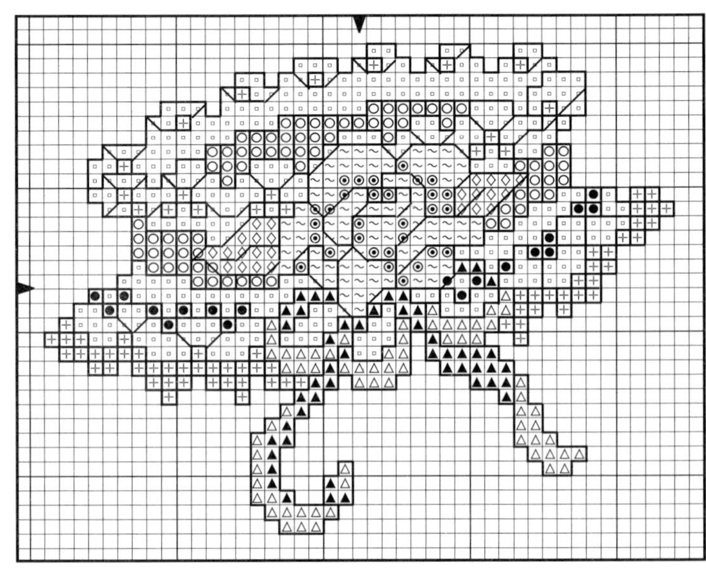

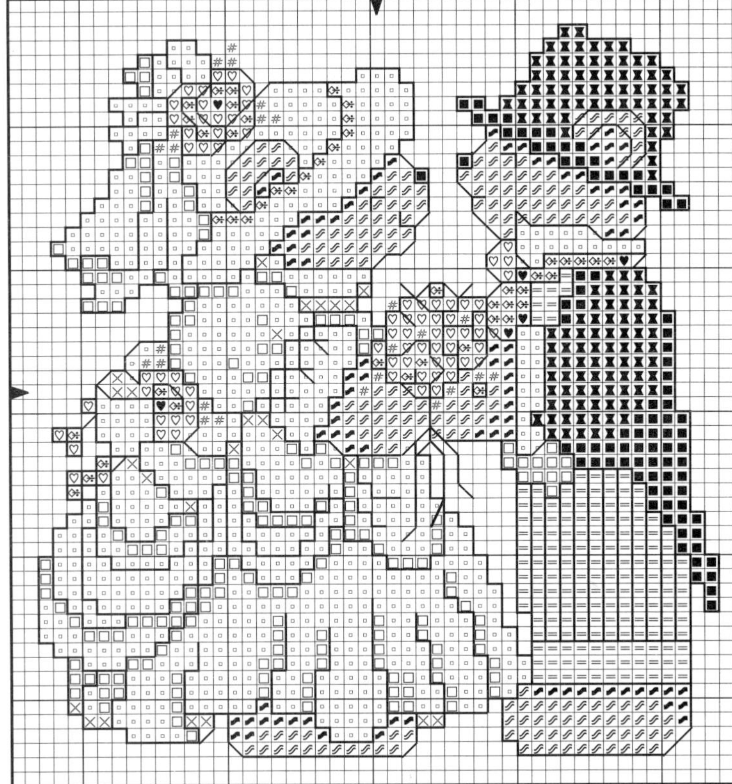

26

Design size: 47 wide x 51 high
Stitching note: If desired, attach a charm (Mill Hill 12116) with a crystal seed bead on bride's hat.

		Anchor	Coats	DMC
▫ =	white	2	1001	blanc
♡ =	lt pink	48	3150	3689
✤ =	med pink	36	3125	3326
♥ =	dk pink	38	3283	961
# =	green	261	6266	989
□ =	lt blue	128	7031	800
× =	med blue	129	7976	809
⁄ =	lt tan	367	5375	738
▰ =	med tan	368	5345	437
= =	lt gray	399	8511	318
	med gray	235	8513	414
⧗ =	dk gray	400	8512	317
■ =	black	403	8403	310

| = Backstitch:
flowers—*dk pink*
stems—*green*
trousers—*dk gray*
eyes, mouths—*black (2 strands)*
remaining outlines—*med gray*

27

Design size: 53 wide x 32 high
Stitching note: If desired, attach a heart charm (Mill Hill 12073) below beaks.

		Anchor	Coats	DMC
▫ =	white	2	1001	blanc
○ =	lt pink	36	3125	3326
● =	dk pink	38	3283	961
★ =	gold	890	2875	729
~ =	blue	1031	7031	3753
	med gray	235	8513	414
⧗ =	dk gray	401	8514	413
■ =	black	403	8403	310

| = Backstitch:
heart, lettering—*dk pink*
swans—*med gray*

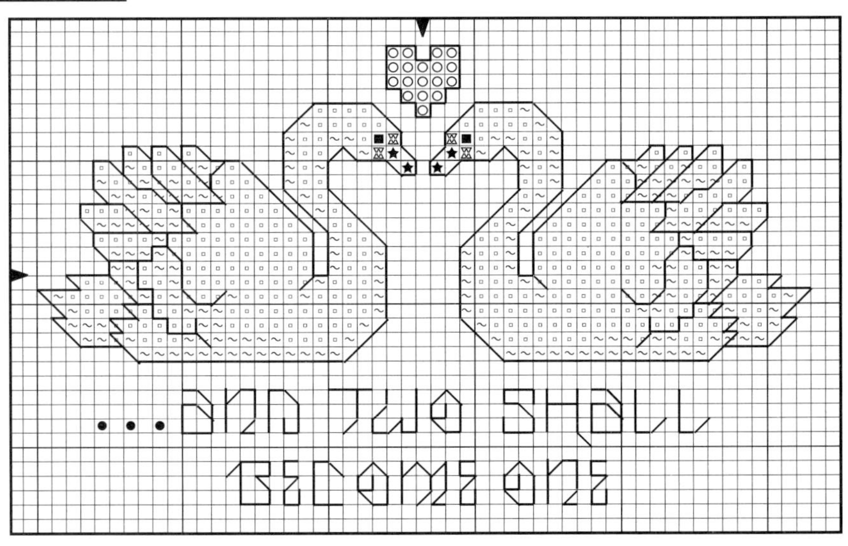

28

Design size: 32 wide x 23 high
Stitching note: Use gold floss to attach beads with 1/2 cross stitches.

			Anchor	Coats	DMC
▫	=	white	2	1001	blanc
☆	=	lt yellow	300	2350	745
★	=	med yellow	891	5363	676
		gold	1001	2308	976
#	=	lt green	240	6016	966
		dk green	243	6239	703
△	=	lt blue	128	7031	800
▲	=	med blue	119	7150	333
♡	=	lt purple	342	4303	211
♥	=	med purple	109	4302	209
		dk purple	112	4300	552
		gray	400	8512	317

Mill Hill Seed Beads

+ = gold 00557

| = Backstitch:
flowers—*gold*
leaves, stems—*dk green*
lettering—*dk purple*
banner, bells—*gray*

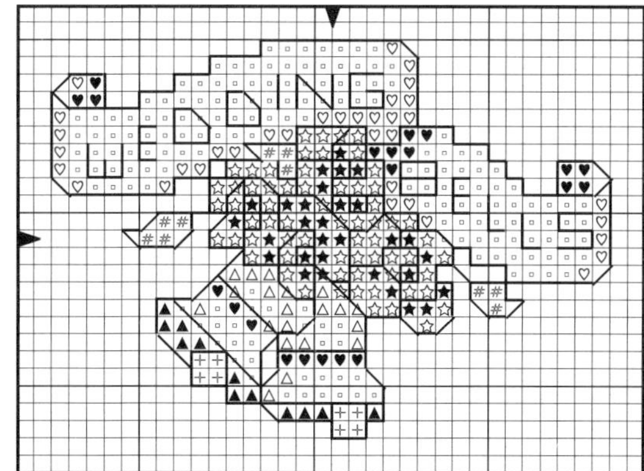

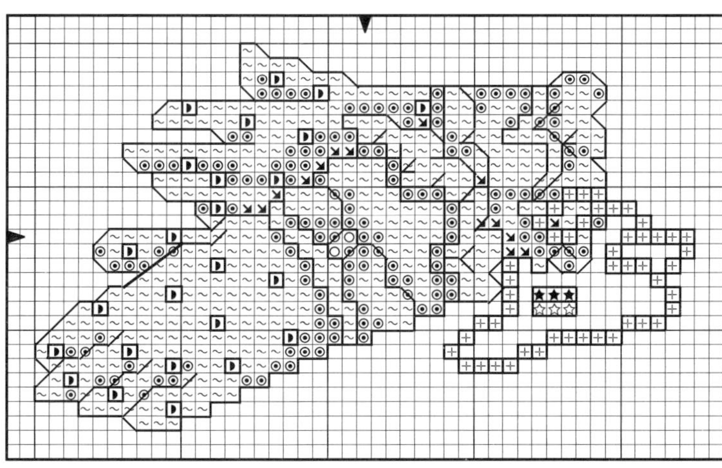

29

Design size: 45 wide x 27 high
Stitching note: Backstitch the square outlines around beads, then use lt cream floss to attach the cream beads with cross stitches, and white floss to attach the white beads with 1/2 cross stitches.

			Anchor	Coats	DMC
		white	2	1001	blanc
~	=	lt cream	885	2386	739
⊙	=	med cream	366	3335	951
➘	=	dk cream	368	5345	437
○	=	lt pink	36	3125	3326
		dk pink	38	3283	961
☆	=	lt gold	311	2305	3827
★	=	med gold	890	2875	729
		dk gold	1001	2308	976
		very dk gold	309	5309	781
		gray	235	8513	414

Mill Hill Seed Beads

+ = white 00479
◗ = cream 00123

| = Backstitch:
jewel—*dk pink*
ring—*dk gold*
gloves—*very dk gold*
bead outlines—*gray*

30

Design size: 47 wide x 40 high
Stitching note: Backstitch the square outlines around beads, then use one strand of white floss to attach beads with 1/2 cross stitches.

			Anchor	Coats	DMC
▫	=	white	2	1001	blanc
✧	=	pink	36	3125	3326
~	=	yellow	301	2293	744
		gold	308	5308	781
⊙	=	blue	128	7031	800
♡	=	purple	342	4303	211
☆	=	tan	368	5345	437
		gray	400	8512	317

Mill Hill Seed Beads

+ = pearl 00479

| = Backstitch:
flower—*gold*
hat, veil, hat stand, bead outlines, bow—*gray*

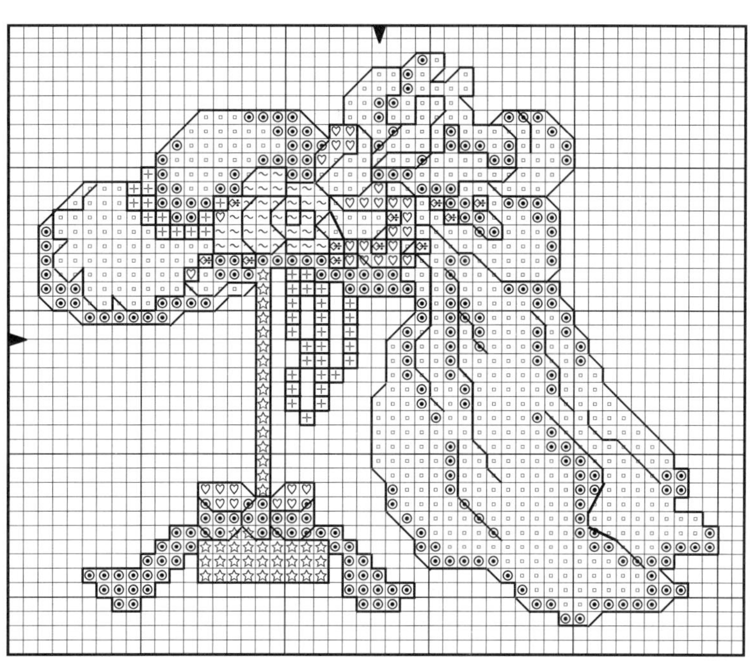

31

Design size: 41 wide x 32 high

Stitching note: If desired, attach a teardrop charm (Mill Hill 13054) at bottom of heart.

		Anchor	Coats	DMC
~ =	pink	48	3150	3689
	rose	76	3176	961
☆ =	lt gold	311	2305	3827
★ =	med gold	890	2875	729
	dk gold	309	5309	781
△ =	lt turquoise	158	7053	747
+ =	med turquoise	186	6185	959
▲ =	dk turquoise	188	6187	3812

| = Backstitch: rings—*dk gold*
heart—*rose* ribbon—*dk turquoise*

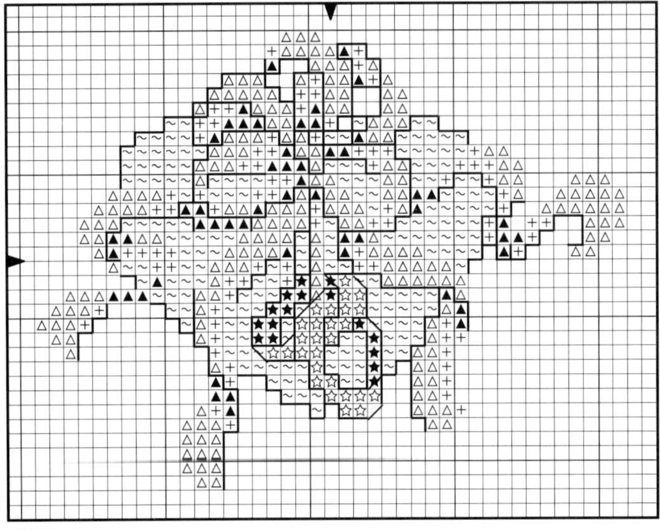

33

Design size: 42 wide x 39 high

Stitching note: If desired, attach a charm (Mill Hill 12010) with a crystal seed bead at center base of fan.

		Anchor	Coats	DMC
▫ =	white	2	1001	blanc
~ =	very lt yellow	275	2275	746
☆ =	lt yellow	300	2350	745
× =	med yellow	301	2293	744
★ =	dk yellow	891	5363	676
➘ =	gold	901	2876	3829

╲ = Straight Stitch: *gold* | = Backstitch: *gold*

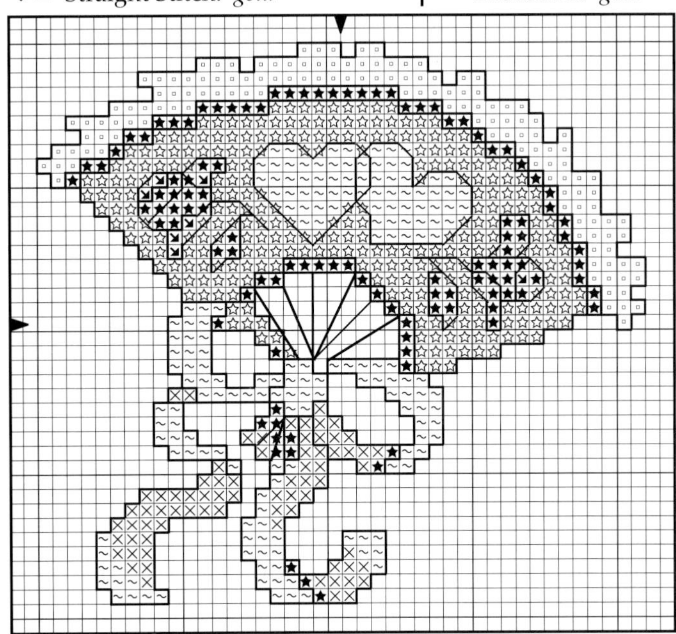

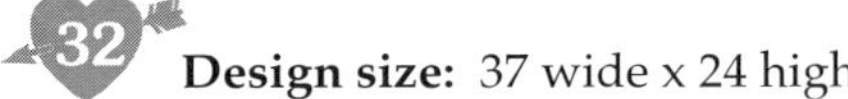

32

Design size: 37 wide x 24 high

		Anchor	Coats	DMC
★ =	gold	307	5307	783
~ =	lt blue	939	7005	794
	med blue	940	7022	792
^ =	lt gray	398	8398	415
⧖ =	dk gray	401	8514	413
■ =	black	403	8403	310

| = Backstitch:
lettering—*med blue*
cane, hat—*black*

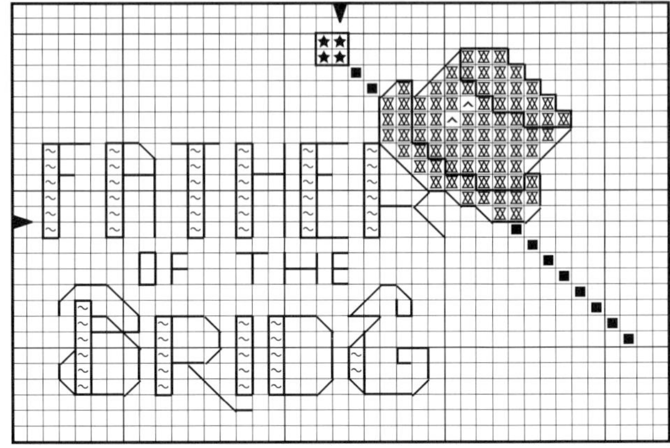

34

Design size: 36 wide x 47 high

Stitching notes: Use the alphabet on page 17 to work desired names with dk turquoise. If desired, attach a teardrop charm (Mill Hill 13053) below bow knot.

		Anchor	Coats	DMC
▫ =	white	2	1001	blanc
○ =	lt pink	48	3150	3689
⊗ =	med pink	36	3125	3326
♡ =	lt turquoise	185	6185	964
♥ =	dk turquoise	187	6186	958
× =	blue	128	7031	800
	gray	235	8513	414

| = Backstitch: turquoise bow—*dk turquoise*
remaining outlines—*gray*

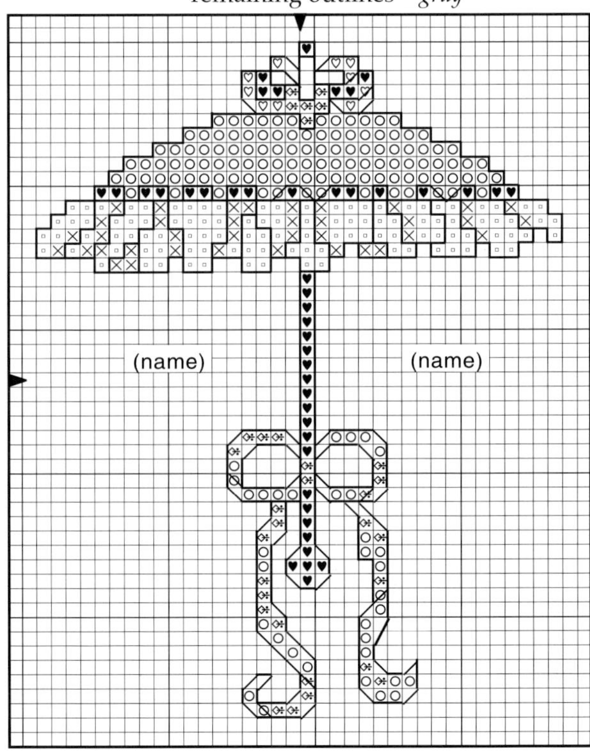

35

Design size: 34 wide x 16 high
Stitching note: Backstitch the square outlines around beads, then use white floss to attach beads with 1/2 cross stitches.

		Anchor	Coats	DMC
	white	2	1001	blanc
♡ =	lt pink	48	3150	3689
	dk pink	38	3283	961
~ =	lt gold	386	2386	3823
✱ =	med gold	891	5363	676
	dk gold	308	5308	781
△ =	lt green	241	6225	966
	dk green	243	6239	703
	gray	235	8513	414

Mill Hill Seed Beads
+ = white 03021

| = Backstitch:
flower—*dk pink*
pin outline, lettering—*dk gold*
stem, leaves—*dk green*
bead outlines—*gray*

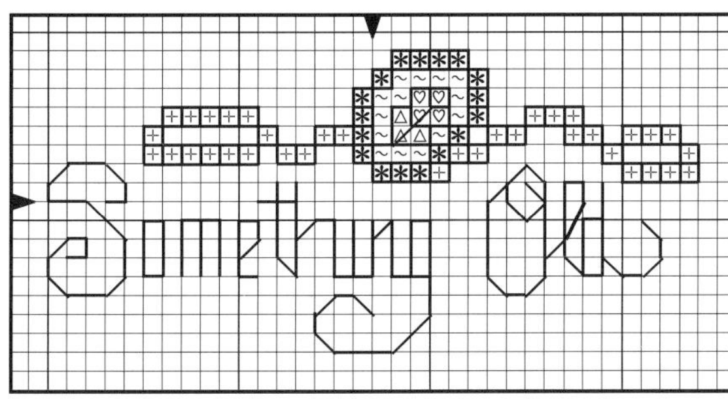

37

Design size: 39 wide x 18 high
Stitching note: Use white floss to attach beads with 1/2 cross stitches.

		Anchor	Coats	DMC
▫ =	white	2	1001	blanc
◈ =	pink	74	3003	3354
◆ =	green	243	6239	703
⊙ =	lt blue	129	7976	809
	med blue	131	7022	798
	gray	235	8513	414

Mill Hill Seed Beads
+ = pearl 00479

| = Backstitch:
stems—*green*
lettering—*med blue*
remaining outlines—*gray*

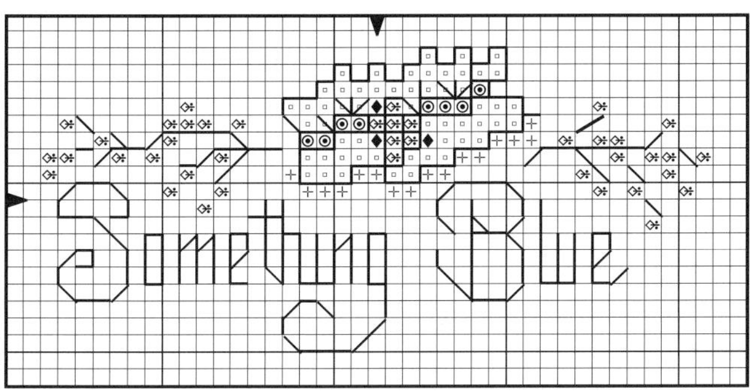

36

Design size: 33 wide x 16 high
Stitching note: Use white floss to attach beads with 1/2 cross stitches.

		Anchor	Coats	DMC
	white	2	1001	blanc
◈ =	fuchsia	96	4104	3609
△ =	lt gold	891	5363	676
	dk gold	307	5307	783
	green	243	6239	703

Mill Hill Seed Beads
× = crystal 02010

| = Backstitch:
ring—*dk gold*
stems, lettering—*green*

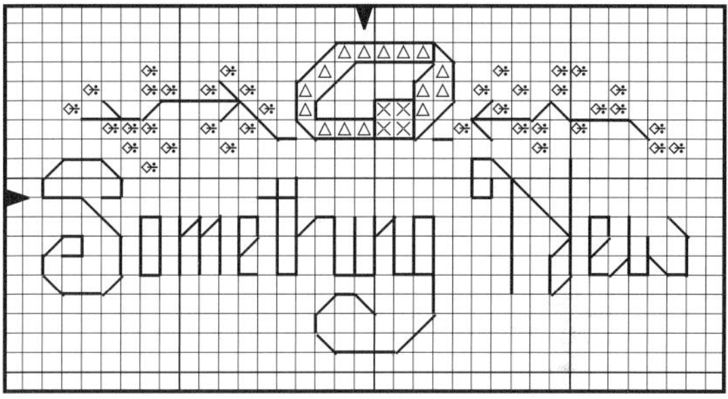

38

Design size: 45 wide x 24 high
Stitching note: Backstitch the square outlines around beads, then use white floss to attach beads with 1/2 cross stitches.

		Anchor	Coats	DMC
▫ =	white	2	1001	blanc
	pink	38	3283	961
~ =	lt peach	6	3006	754
◢ =	dk peach	9	3008	352
	green	243	6239	703
◈ =	blue	128	7031	800
	gray	235	8513	414

Mill Hill Seed Beads
+ = pearl 00479

| = Backstitch:
flower, lettering—*pink*
leaves—*green*
bead outlines, bag, ribbon—*gray*

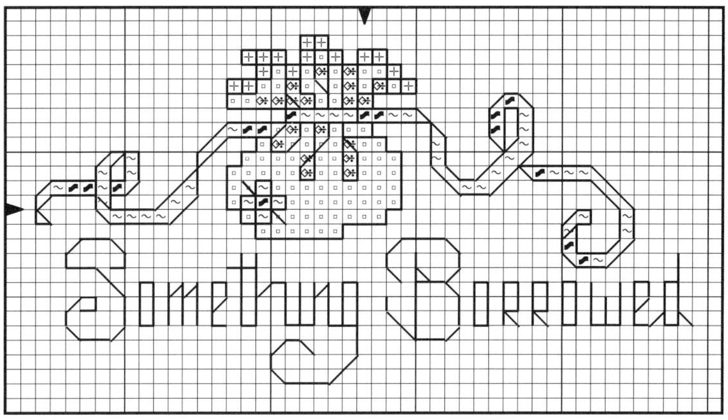

39

Design size: 35 wide x 42 high
Stitching note: Use one strand of white floss to attach beads with 1/2 cross stitches.

		Anchor	Coats	DMC
▫ =	white	2	1001	blanc
○ =	lt pink	48	3150	3689
⟡ =	med pink	74	3003	3354
● =	dk pink	76	3176	961
☆ =	yellow	300	2350	745
◇ =	lt green	203	6030	564
	dk green	230	6031	699
× =	blue	129	7976	809
∞ =	purple	96	4104	3609
	gray	235	8513	414

Mill Hill Seed Beads

+ =	gold	00557

| = Backstitch:
lettering—*dk pink*
leaves, stems—*dk green*
chapel, ribbon, bells, flowers—*gray*

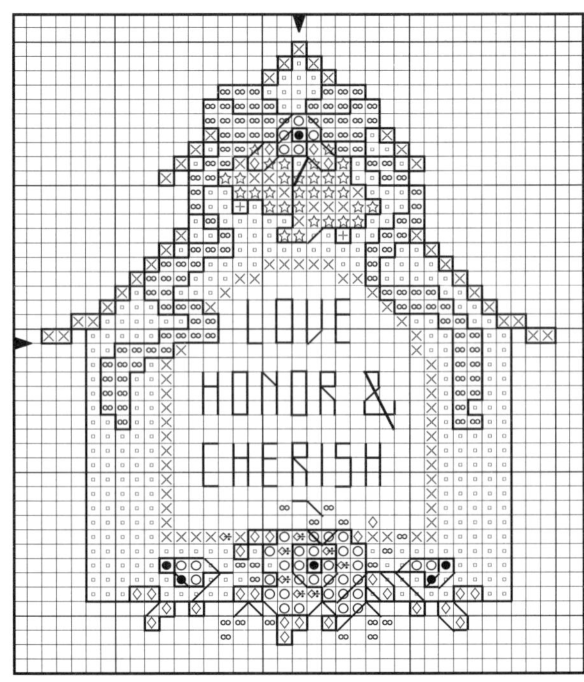

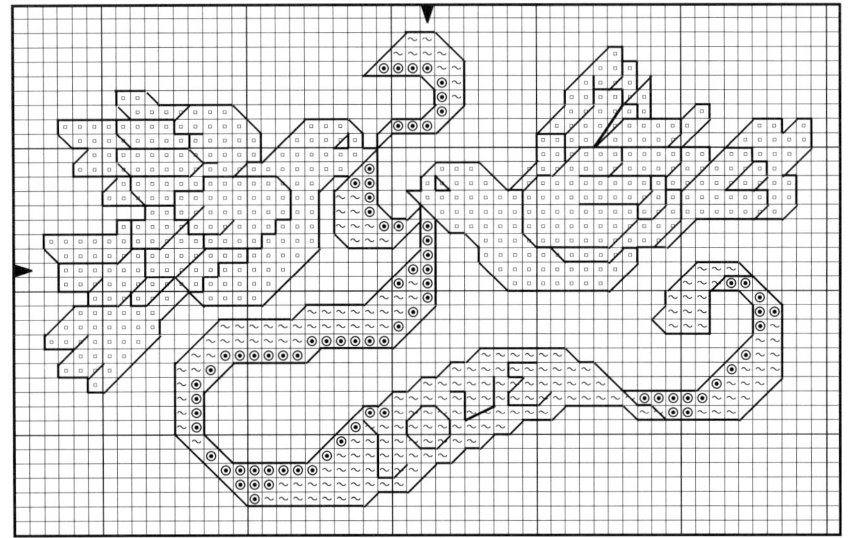

40

Design size: 53 wide x 33 high
Stitching note: If desired, attach a teardrop charm (Mill Hill 13055) on ribbon.

		Anchor	Coats	DMC
▫ =	white	2	1001	blanc
~ =	ivory	275	2275	746
⊙ =	lt gold	891	5363	676
	dk gold	309	5309	781
	blue	131	7022	798

| = Backstitch:
banner—*dk gold*
doves, lettering—*blue*

41

Design size: 40 wide x 41 high
Stitching note: Use blue floss to attach lilac beads and purple floss to attach purple beads, all with cross stitches.

		Anchor	Coats	DMC
▫ =	white	2	1001	blanc
⟡ =	med pink	33	3012	3706
● =	dk pink	35	3152	3801
~ =	peach	1012	2331	754
☆ =	lt gold	361	5375	738
© =	med gold	363	5351	436
	dk gold	370	5356	434
	green	877	6878	3815
	blue	136	7030	799
	purple	97	4097	554
◗ =	rust	1013	2338	3778
	gray	235	8513	414

Mill Hill Seed Beads

+ =	lilac	02009
^ =	purple	00252

| = Backstitch:
pistils, cross—*dk gold*
stems, lettering—*green*
flowers—*gray*

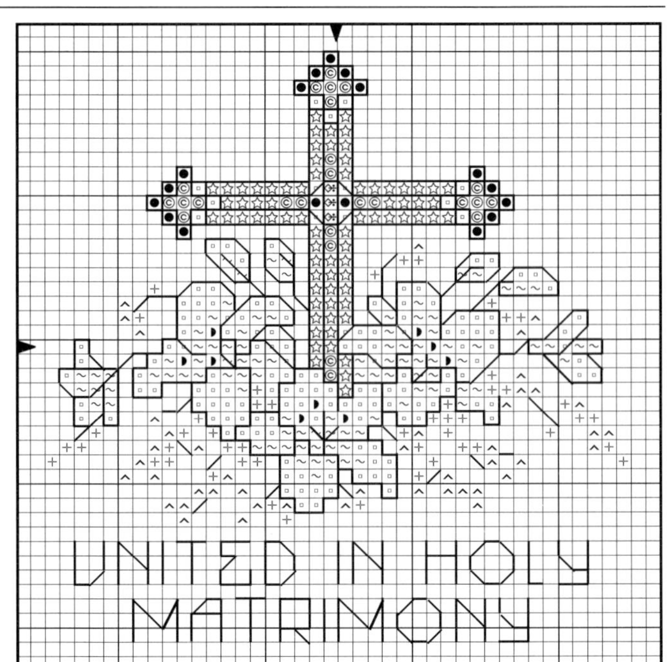

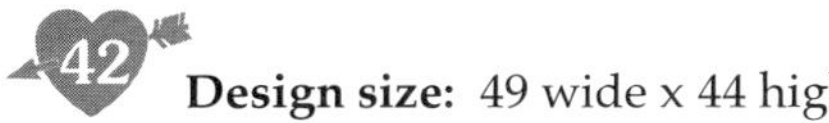

Design size: 49 wide x 44 high

Symbol	Color	Anchor	Coats	DMC
○ =	lt pink	74	3003	3354
● =	dk pink	76	3176	961
~ =	lt peach	8	3868	3824
	dk peach	10	3011	351
☆ =	lt yellow	300	2350	745
	dk yellow	313	2302	742
◇ =	lt green	206	6209	564
	med green	204	6210	563
	blue	1038	7168	519
	purple	97	4097	554

| = Backstitch:
pink & peach flower petals—*dk pink*
"M," "Ri"—*dk pink (2 strands)*
peach & yellow flower petals—*dk peach*
"oth," "de"—*dk peach (2 strands)*
stems, leaves, leaf veins—*med green*
"er," "of," branch, tendrils—*med green (2 strands)*
"th"—*blue (2 strands)*
remaining "e," "B"—*purple (2 strands)*

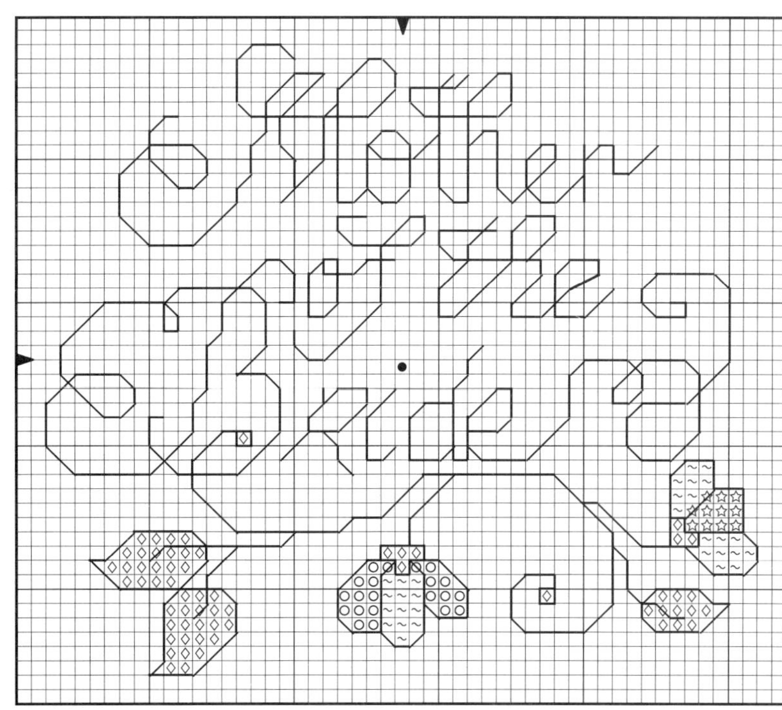

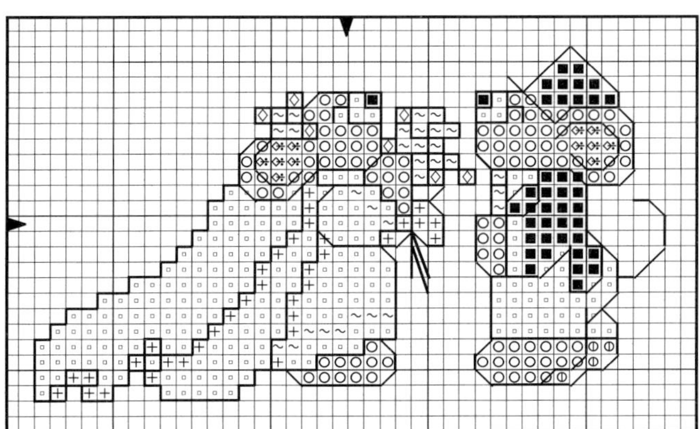

Design size: 40 wide x 23 high

Symbol	Color	Anchor	Coats	DMC
▫ =	white	2	1001	blanc
⊕ =	pink	73	3173	963
~ =	peach	8	3868	3824
◇ =	lt green	214	6016	368
	dk green	205	6205	912
+ =	blue	128	7031	800
○ =	lt gray	397	8397	3024
Φ =	med gray	398	8398	415
■ =	dk gray	400	8512	317

╲ = Straight Stitch: *dk green*
| = Backstitch: *dk gray*

44

Design size: 43 wide x 41 high
Stitching notes: Use the alphabet on page 17 to work desired names with dk blue. If desired, attach a heart charm (Mill Hill 12073) over heart at base of tree.

Symbol	Color	Anchor	Coats	DMC
▫ =	white	2	1001	blanc
○ =	lt pink	36	3125	3326
● =	dk pink	38	3283	961
~ =	peach	778	2336	3774
☆ =	yellow	891	5363	676
◇ =	lt green	240	6016	966
	dk green	210	6213	562
□ =	lt blue	128	7031	800
	dk blue	131	7022	798
⟐ =	rust	1047	5347	402
△ =	lt gray	398	8398	415
▲ =	dk gray	235	8513	414

| = Backstitch:
mouths, boutonniere—*dk pink*
tree stems, leaves—*dk green*
lettering—*dk blue*
remaining outlines—*dk gray*

(name) (name)

45 **Design size:** 81 wide x 19 high

Stitching notes: Use the alphabet on page 17 to work desired names with med turquoise. Use white floss to attach pearl beads with 1/2 cross stitches and med gold floss to attach gold beads with cross stitches.

		Anchor	Coats	DMC
▫	= white	2	1001	blanc
✧	= pink	75	3001	962
☆	= lt gold	300	2350	745
★	= med gold	891	5363	676
^	= lt turquoise	185	6185	964
⊙	= med turquoise	187	6186	958
	gray	235	8513	414

		Mill Hill Seed Beads
+	= pearl	00479
*	= gold	00557

| = Backstitch: *gray*

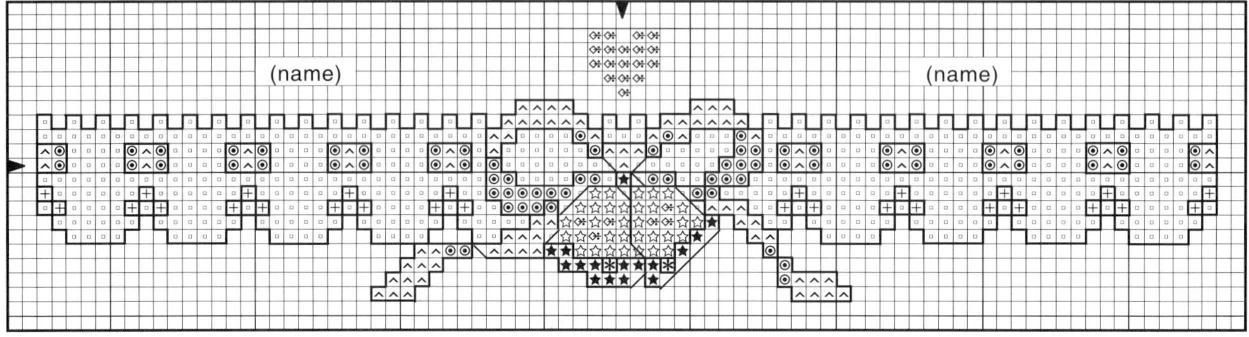

46 **Design size:** 26 wide x 15 high

		Anchor	Coats	DMC
▫	= white	2	1001	blanc
○	= lt pink	73	3173	963
✧	= med pink	75	3001	962
–	= very lt green	847	6005	3072
#	= med green	240	6016	966
^	= tan	366	3335	951
	gray	400	8512	317

| = Backstitch: *gray*

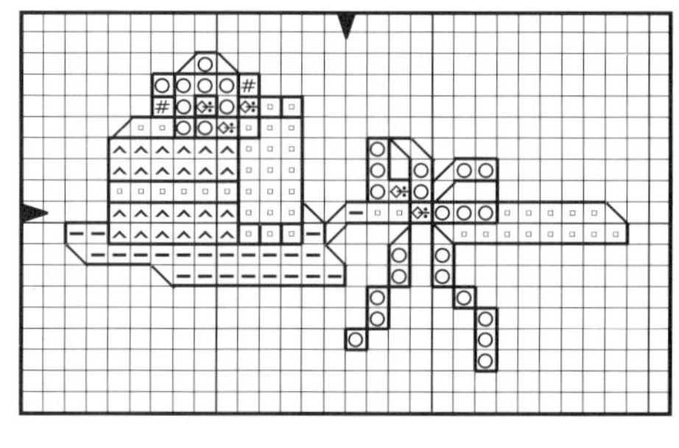

47 **Design size:** 77 wide x 34 high

		Anchor	Coats	DMC
○	= lt pink	48	3150	3689
✧	= med pink	36	3125	3326
●	= dk pink	38	3283	961
~	= lt peach	6	3006	754
⊙	= med peach	9	3008	352
↘	= dk peach	10	3011	351
☆	= lt yellow	300	2350	745
★	= med yellow	301	2293	744
◇	= lt green	1043	6015	369
#	= med green	240	6016	966
	dk green	210	6213	562

| = Backstitch:
pink flowers—*dk pink*
peach flower, ribbon, lettering—*dk peach*
leaves, tendrils—*dk green*

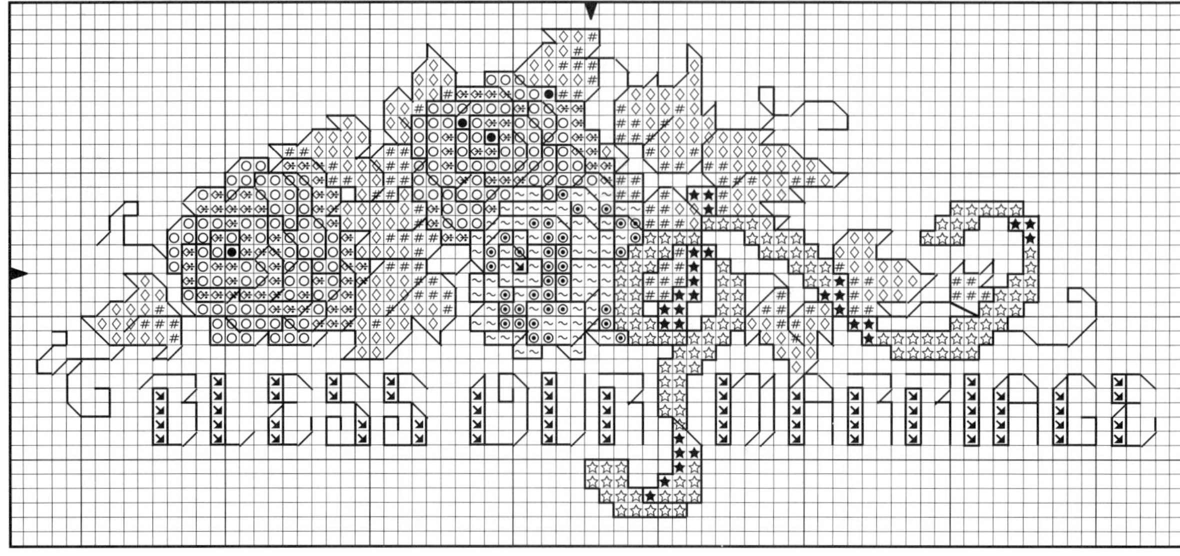